T E T H

T E T H

Sheila E. Murphy

CHAX PRESS   TUCSON 1991

Chax Press is located at 101 West Sixth Street, no. 4, Tucson, Arizona 85701, where, as a member of the Steinfeld Warehouse Cooperative, it shares the historic warehouse. We are grateful to many for their support of the publication of this book, including the National Endowment for the Arts, the Tucson/Pima Arts Council, Bookman's Used Books, and the Chax Press Members.

ISBN 0-925904-05-8

Library of Congress Cataloging-in-Publication Data
Murphy, Sheila E., 1951-
      Teth / Sheila Murphy.
                  p.   cm.
      Poetry.
      ISBN 0-925904-05-8   : $9.00
      I. Title.
PS3563.U7618T48   1991
811'.54--dc20   90-48157
                                                                      CIP

Sheila Murphy's Grace

Sheila Murphy compels repetition, invites it, precisely because what she repeats is an action, the sitting down with the mind alive to all that's around (and to a human mind much of "what's around" will sound abstract but is as present as the pepper) as here her "Impala/parked halfway in drive" becomes as thought about yet another Transcendental as in Emerson emblem. Em as in Murphy. Thoreau would like it that her refrigerator "transforms/poached pear into fiberglass" and yet these are very much the act of writing, not moving *toward* priveleged moments, acrylic aperçus but being going where they are. To do this ingenuously is the thing, the knack, the project, without false naivety or tinny sophistication, ragtime throwaway. She says "my harmonica's abrasive thumbtone" and it's definitive but not unclumsy, in fact abrasive as are her next two or three verbs. This being hard on yourself to write well is very like self-hate. Her Tethiness: the one beginning "borscht akimbo" is heady as a jazz riff in its centered motions down to "temporary jaded silo" which I don't think's so nice and what is it to save a thing, "finish" it unless you allow flatnesses, denying yourself the effect of effect? Not the wrong word but the nonword, word purely as spacer (this now needs a word like this) will come in here, as people like Murphy really like the phrase as a thing different from a word and prior. What her eye falls on, kites, clothespins, record jackets, gets in but not (so much) as diurnal notation, this because this-then, but as a religious trusting of the perceptual manifold to be an Event. Sheila E. Murphy.

I like how religious considerations come in in these, "spell disrepair" a spell in disrepair, little dirge on religion gone to old pressed disk. The horrible unwritten poem on being thought pregnant at the checkout counter becomes "long distance breastmilk" unless that's a last fillip, anyway mothers are in it and her relation to the mother in her in a way that tricks you nicely, more richly than its magazine shadow. There's almost Zukofskyan domesticity to "here where thought culls", pretty phrase a sandwich with the next's "the sensibility of the professor beside/open questions"— she's handling what we're to do with fine phrases here. And music runs through these like *Ulysses*. Sheila E. Bloom. She may be writing them in exam books, "the dismal/Thursday kind of blue" as she's written of rubber bands, string drawer of the mind, from no being at a loss. When her writing goes slack it's the verbs that go not the nouns. This is probably true of very good writers; for others the noun is a subject. Since *With House Silence* she's liked a line like a jumbled shelf—peace winter corrugated homelife—that sits like Thoreau chairs outdoors. Or writing in heaven, "better answers than amenities/in approximate stiff endpoint." I so liked *endpoint* it took a minute to see how good "approximate stiff" is, how unapproximate, except in the way "approximate" wanders into the next word, straitens or transforms itself to it. Which is to say two words in Sheila Murphy are a little plot, as "equal a range heals" runs on its inserted words to make a globe patently projection. There's always a grace somewhere. (The love poems are breathtaking.) Is Sheila radiant. She sums things in "not to announce" without summing *up* (Sheila E. Maugham). Her plots are yachts, "yacht floats" on French genders, as if *How to Write* includes a Punch and Judy script. Weave and throw pots. Warlords submit to quiet, "and light stood often still/awaiting dance form" how meditation is in these poems, not even as a medium but as outside transparency to which writing acts refer. Illumination is writing's due; "sidebar/of the only music is beyond/only the music" says she, and "what do you make of/one mascara colored sock/left in the middle street" in which two words are lovely, one absent. Survey Roget, she says, and ends with "pepper enough colored to depress/paprika over chicken" which I submit for depress, the use of the single word a vivid joke, motion of the cook's wrist writing. A word is maternal in her, at worst a translation from a situation into a thing, but a word's so much an action for her that her associations are kinesthetic, play ball! and one does. The stretching body includes a womb, quasiinertial anchor felt by pivoting at hip, "the muscle expectations" expectations.

Gerald Burns

for Beverly Carver

insinuate a thing must dream itself
woven in snow
apparently the guise of Gable
may I have this
relocation please
shovels and crew assignments
spelling bee glitch chemlab
exploit leave
to glean how much they loved you
sacrifice for verity
the nymphomaniac circumference of love
stilted unruly body television
unmarked police hum blended virtue
genuflect
the theater has precedence
over some certain sacraments
temperate enough to happen
by themselves
air in sufficient tires
to guide the road regarding
its true place

familiar breath
familiar brown doorpaint
familiar cavities on sidewalk moving muscles
cleave serenely orbits
thought to be apologies for dirt
mingled intention
water as a ceiling
folds the architect into a bloom
serious keyboard covering
the lids we dapple to detain us
or precede ontology
the hyphen blindly corresponding
to nightmare with a hole
embedded seriously filled
with round dimensional light
and savings majesty
would dream some overage
the Mormon storage of supplies
high on continuance
if not purely the self

virgin prophet indigo quite deep eyes
manufactures pain
from which he'll rescue
meanwhile the relief
impresses only lean mauve veering
on white walls
comfortably enough
to be a present tense
the recent past like war
all heroes have dismantled
as rug fibers handmade
then sequestered
name your planet henceforth
rise to the occasion
violet tufts
immaculate cream skin
as pretense heralds for the comfortable soul
first home enunciated thirst
luster and chimney nestled
as the signals branch
toward an unclaimed sea

abacus along
the memory page
delete add
fraction of indifference
host where remedy
seeps white round nodules
beneath the tongue
philosophy secretes
what screen intends
disuse entangles photograph
with what the witness saw
sufficient room
to seem at home in
carnivore depleting
gentleness
the way the flower situation
comes to dumpling
count them
each measure of breeze
rest foraging
for bare essentials
in our home resultant struggle
how the mainframe rescues
what reluctantly we have released
to certain wind on empty

day's work not control
would serve epistemology's return light
we abuse or move the body
past its work of planting
hybrid lapdog mere surrender
portion slush and chipseal
envy through weekly divisive countdown
serendipity I love you
fossil wheatcake
love you alabaster
this outmoded pigeon
at my crossing vestibule
the simple heat
to a condition medical supplies
can waste into oblivious cold places
near the stars white lazy
for our lenses and a well known spice
to change appearance even spine

auto androgeny Impala
parked halfway in drive
ejection home
his forward motion
permanent drive
relaxed
parked with companion
genuinely frost free evening
biology impales itelf on habit
a release of expectation
confirmation of the pattern
endless saving crypt
of answers vantage pointed wax job
motioning to spirit
to become a body
anyway
enjoy prelude to rope burns
prefiguring the severance
handsomely
an interest in reconstructing
shape and teeth and smile
after predictable enough action
motioning exhibit to attendees
of the exhibition

Sparta wakes heaven in my hand
things fall from verbs
the only man I ever courted seriously
modeled the downfall of parental love
the self in hiding
homoerotic consequence in gallery
a plenty stippled grievance
to emit sachet
blue tranquil modesty
like hints of sleep
in snoring tapestry on tapestry
midwife alleging what it is that happened yesterday
exactly this much slack
to fend off rivals with bare rope
folded perfectly
to meet the neck that segregates
the mind from form

refrigerator transforms
poached pear
into fiberglass
all winter
wanted distributive
warm socks noble endurance
traditional in season
ever perjuring
anomaly from happening
the blue discursive incident
so blond it's truly happy
misspelling from hell appliances
significant difference at the .05 level
my harmonica's abrasive thumbtone
patriots are out of style
their schoolwork is infested
with numb logic don't forget
to request a transfer then
remember to get out after remembering
to pull the cord tell the driver story of line
segment

borscht akimbo during vodka
I remember freedom
looking through the wavy glass
water pressure
clean remark
professor chapped and bald
seeking the adoration
of lean mineral experience
hometown street pinch
something of real life
amend routine pleasure a comb
small frame
to exhaust perspective
chance redemption
be prepared to lose
the whole investment
guarantee
a 25% return
the golf entreaty joyride
slender tip light
until bathtub ignites the warm club
fifty anything in round numbers
manipulate sweet cauldron
temporary jaded silo

looking inward is a mountain
of accepted change
the change no poltergeist
habitual intrusion
scuffs the nurture impulse
symphony we pay for wails
to be at home
to be defined
as flute a gravity approval
seeks variety
the legislative clothespins
bask in full star presence
as a blue kite sailing
through flipside darkness
from the polar opposite
as spillage glistens from the pooltracks
GretL evidence across an aging deck
awakens feet to locate a position
most to savor during neutral heat

leave me a quiet will
the things of yours I want
a non-denominational long day
translating the discovered mystics
breeding world from raw resources
newspaper a precursor of papier-mache
solutions to divestiture
dysfunction leaning etiquette
on stampface
scrapbook mention of the reason
people go in droves to campsites
where pretend indulgence
in the lesser things
transpires out-take
rocks me to sleep
until the spirit
drifts into elapsed seafoam
and musters a correlative
for lower back
without something pending
the sore places

mildly newpaperish lingo
snares wan span of attention
is plasma the target
what blood
semiotic worthy cause
repeated course in courses
lavish little snare drums
poised to cover the philanthropy
this land needs happen
to fall victim to diversion
a full head of rockband hair
cinquains garbled over
questionable sound system
imitating full release
of mind glued on
after amazing amplitude
the forest greentones laden
with full day
knowingly caught mid-sentence
with ruins of near answers
long play
instead of disc

spell disrepair
perform the expectations
major winter learns to climb
a distance
with the name *taut string*
that could be member of quintet
but is a solitude
resourceful as the nimble monk
forming disuse
of his feeble ingredients
announced lessons
in how to plagiarize good health
of someone relevant
the deejays spin quantity
devalue alms
contort their stores of ammunition
transcribed into signatures
well recognized
expound on divinity
as a companion
exercise in free will
one of several
oiled vintage choices

mahatma fox I call her reverentially
as gladiator forces evil their intention
in pursuit of home to me
demystify the scoundrels
sanctifying blood
they use to dye their clothes
at a tremendous cost per wearing
in contrast to her one
froth colored soul extension
a persuasive emblem of interior
reflect rejection syntax
even as it blushes so bystanders
if they do exist can view
and draw conclusive
sustenance plaited
and fully soothed somewhere
within the riddle
no one has to pose

long distance breastmilk
unrequited symptom
holy swimming pool menagerie
the pilgrim children never mine
menstrual cavity resolved
again societal detention
the one instance
I bought baby food for us
a vegetarian simplific spree
enclave of easy
for the weeks that we could stand
no sodium at all
no interest
they smiled warmly
from cash register
less to my cash
than a condition fictive
being wanted by a stranger
and redeemed for her
a mother to me anyone
allow me to self-introduce

here where thought culls
chaste ink blank enough
wash brim gleam clear through
razor
shift the neutral balance
hear me speak
to self unmet
how smooth and perfect is the sell
how mellow can the decade be
in return
true feeling burns off purity
like smudge around this house
gleans sounds without the enmity
confused dim recreational
crazed self
rinses coconut from hungover skin
a tap on shoulder
invades the blur she has transisted
to the surprising open mountains
hoping welcome

third person singular object
in the subject place
so audible it stings
"her and I went to the language lab"
etcetera
lung pressure sanctifies
a marble base
on which unkempt statues
are weaned of adoration
caliber of thin priests
mortarboard
stifle the wish
and swollen glands of separatists
lonely for edges
quietly defined
trim shore then feast on motion
sanctifying grace pours down like blood
wholly identified
bereft of blisters
enable thunder near
the sensibility of the professor beside
open questions

critique how I make love
is simple yet reliving miniblooms
a sliver open foremost
the attention focused on some light
the weight and feel of melody
newborn tangent to ingenious interlocutor
meander sift the whole precipitation
smother highlight enough dream
to cushion palace hibernation
into jealous form of astral travel
ever untamed majesty
the courtroom graduation moments
to anticipate policeman's ointment
then a clarinet without visual image
scraping any sky
doing its fistful of elated tandem
toward the end plenty immaculate

commandments shirk their duty to be open
close up the imposing shop
snap pictures
of the faithful lined up
outside window
with a "closed" sign
a reminder sanctity is courage
not adherence to the rules
and travail
hammer the disuse of self
into unworthy frame
refrigerator offers to regret
being alive
the oven reluctantly agrees
to collude in freeing
house of prayer from wiretap
god already listens to
phonetics
beams license fees to earth
and faxes sentiment
awkward or simply
unpronounceable

symphonic breeze I really see
those optical illusions
think them
real corridors of mention
the hypotenuse
of charm relates its bruises
to the perpetrators of self bruising
warns
of too delicious privacy
for clarity gemstones anoint
fingers discoverers
waste cans
pressure how we lived
to answer hopeless questions
like the furnace in hot season
keep the functional a breath
away from dying
sliver the remains
and share the sifted ruins
of thin screens
in wide awake new audience
with name rings

per our agreement thistling
mo-mantra fresh Montmartre the metro tube
this river of my neck
mind wizened coal shock of the cheekbone
shave and shore alike
say blink
the man semester hides
in blue book
it is the dismal
Thursday kind of blue
kings wish were drought occasionally
consistently the tucked in frame
alongside risk
newborn repeat signs
surname hemline blood
pose cleared for prescient creekbed
pathing trance into a keepsake
trembles cave of small print
telepathic art museum
fully vested

the little depot with some moss in it
had many passengers
and friends who wanted mention
in the walls to be forgiveness
every lift of luggage tabled
some ongoing conversation
for a breath
enough to squeeze out gravity
from motion
without declaring sides within the body
temperature
nearly defeated
sweet on caliber of death
meaning enchantment
of the rising kind
apprentice means when mist white peonies appear
to take attention from the fingers
second guessing soil
and likely quality of blossom

tome is wisecrack sketched alive
say intuition bore resemblance
to an audience
created of its wisdom
purge straitjacketed proforma
dizzy with untimely lack of rescue
muscleshirting its way
into the voting crowd
of bright light habitat
the register plumb saturated
with maternity
as a for instance
to dismember stations of the cross
memory bank plenty symmetrical
with shabby out-takes
glass persona ritually personal
all saved ahead as green stamps
could be licked into a book
exchanged for a Corvette or something

civilization forms blind culture
we are sifted to prevent
an elemental elegance
think of mystics
infinitely strangers
reflect the industry of paradise
our legs talented run away
nudge cupboards
they close things
we have amassed
no longer think of sharing
hierarchy places baldness above elbows
we feel forced to stay atop
intend to get also beneath
when level is the corresponding eye
peace winter corrugated homelife
this furniture
perfectly simple
you can lift it
go away
and be constantly
at home

violet colored violets
in rich soil over the white rug
synonym for happiness
breed boy and give him accolades
some near nirvana pension to anticipate
he tosses blooming plants away
like Chevrolet paint
when his muscles haven't owned a car in years
the syncopated ashtray ready for donations
though untouched
the holy ghost residual guess work
weigh station
comatose contingency
routinely pressing nerves and being thickly nerves
androgynous alliance
a candle pleasing
catechism axe
to ponder any wavering
reduction or enlargement

monarch butterfly
opaque enough to lift me
lift me named shift
thinking people change
from tyranny
proving syllables do
do not contain
a pressure to be thinking
hardwood in them ashen
tone complexion
shut down quiet promenade of images
train veering from a central corridor
to where all birds in conscience flow
what will our evolution be
from this space
to accept a foreign cryptic license
lacing steps as traffic pours down easy
better answers than amenities
in approximate stiff endpoint

equal a range heals
by her measured pacing
mutual accomplishment
tack pictures of success to walls
things happen
gospel music moderately priced
percussive chillblains
expectorating national health care
need broken diskette ridiculous extremes
sea bass a sphere flattened
at the poles discrepancies
a picturebook blue lines
reading to me
I try to paint the very brush outdated map
I listen to vocal critic
kneepop as she rises
to accept significance
of a geography
published before the turn
rounding another continent bystander

canoe shaped heaven
icicles dismantled
why don't you send your congressman a wave
of bundled serum
how many snakebites do the Eskimos imagine
being heard of Cheshire face
canary simple waterway
the blessed chemistry
of indoor pictures flash caress
and simplex
heavy lofty gem of proof
they are together
open birdcage in the center dream
court fraction glide
or something bookish
tantrumed oval
with sufficient finish biochemistry
mind light over the preferred great lake
about to be tame inland
for vacation

rampion he called her
banjoed what venerable rejoinder
he could manage to careen from
insular
as a woman is
career to hunger
sexual starvation
the prescriptive windlace measure
gravity and rise
her nectar of event
his jasmine only desert prey
often a curve of wind
only the hammock smooth awayness
certain cavity a sometime spool
plex portrait haven
jamming oceans down
a songster's wide imagination
purpose mouths words and gravy
words all penmanshipped away
on holiday greatly amended
fluvial certain greatness

not supernatural carefully endorses
windburn soul with ink
webbed curiosity
smokes thirst
when Jane the pregnant charity
bleeds dust
her chafing spirit
stuns portions of map
the grace and light or truth
whose instrument would coalesce
and hamper bits of clogged
or ample self
and furniture the altar sometimes
ornery
intended wealth spills
coffee table chairs upturned
that grovel for space
stalk its firm delusions
oceans of acre dry
acres of open
to moist public gratitude
and longitude a choreography
meantime

is she radiant
oh plenty plenty
she remakes me
at my sincere request
I sometimes glean
when frame shops form the portrait
make an offer
push collective fork
into the food
collective wine
I serve them palpable
with more future results
the mysteries all solve themselves
and partake channel osmotic center spree
let me then sleep beside her temperature
symphony also capable
of infinite informance
this room is pet once
though I digress beyond peyote
open the radio and speak back

learn the womb can't love
enough
select a new
ill-fitting section of the planet
to reside in
claim your heart
frost legged ready to be tried
searing the disappointment
of failed bakery
consistently on empty
holy thistle
on the law
most sanctified
longhand bouquet
mesmeric charity
with glitter still residing
in the comb
whose bristles score some touchdown
like variable plantation mummies
held responsible for apprenticed crops
depressive until certain hunger
she ventriloquist amazingly
appoints herself guru
of failed light
supposing

gendarmes inside remember
proper place
shell crypt pose dangerous
bloodstream
torn to years voiced adios arrangements
norm and silo
classic feather of a man
preponderance
grilled lambent
alloy hock
and poll pop fictive strum
the baste is twitching
in the zero yard unruly pep
diseased and atrophied
part cocker and part rain
slyly composed of imperfection
sealant or developments inimitable
next door features avenue
plantain whose hunger
loose changed daylights
into something mental like a porchlight
in the sentence he illumined

tavern a home
which one of us is portable
insist something
transferable in liquid language
I say tears replicate
one hundred something proof
the lattice work amending
rigorous though barely
trembling narrative
a pair of options
handlebars appear to move
in unified direction
sacrament is knowing
how to translate
leisure to a spiritual work
so punctual the dim sun
lays down a good portion of life
to serve purely a schedule of weather
fully vested stones
and nearby water
spiking history

maybe we project our little village
onto philanthropic squares
of canvas obbligato
temple mention
zoom lens
racial prejudice
award winning concupiscence
I wake tomorrow
my dilemmas solidly intact
tight fitting reasonable assurances
that there will be a day
the mystics cry for untapped
amazing hemisphere
raw face
unleavened muscular control
blurred scope of inference
crazy germane boy resonance
his helper
cryptic cipher jellybean
mind you devalued currency
at last entrepreneurial
resisting the temptation
to cease being prideful
small
informed of consequence

leaves I have attracted
smell of burning
neighborly swing rhythm
lingers past several deaths
their breath hangs neatly
in wide open afternoon
blinking on-again off-again
impending snowstorm
light for inner comfort
after sacrifice hones weather
the prevailing mood
stone personality of light
whose photograph appears
in magazines diverse
as *Popular Woodworking*
Arizona Highways
Better Homes and G
this music speaks in violin
bassoon and steel guitar
to ambidextrous sightseeing
still using mirror
as the prime criterion for beauty
trusting simple vision

not to announce or safen
cover tracks of what I've said
to let the thing be fully
as I hold still
and exact identity
the same as breath
the same as breeze
light weather same
in a dark room
this wood painting
watercolor film
pervasive sleep in paying
quick attention planet
planet ingredient
whole butterfly
exhaust the soft milk episode
in-basket gift
simple assurance
here a piece of jewelry
embossed slavish desire
appearing melody occurs
and breaches semblance
kind oval emerging

preambular morning
if I speak to melody around me
dump truck
slaphappy birds
exhaust
some weakly snarling pets
uncoffeed humans
sponge headphones
pleat the sense of hearing
grapefruit imperceptibly fall juicy over lawns
divestiture the headlock
ounces me in sensibility
live antenna branches
fortify lawn minerals at night ahead
core epoch seethes pronouncement
morning glory sifts edges
of impostor ruins
voice chain link protection
from the mass without possession
of enough imagination to transcend
sound
corrupted how the mind is
music

starts to ease off
then becomes quiet enough
afternoon
leaves like crisp clenched hand
cymbals in the shape of jagged leaves
go dancing
fortitude dog-eared
cryptic falsehood
guessed at stickers
tick of the watch
apprenticed to be
swingset in the deep conundrum
all-day spree
throw a pot and sing
slosh paint across billboards
practice reed near wind
being the lace
brushstrokes above steam
selected paradise breeze by
several birds
whose hunger shrill
a past isosceles endorsement
of the insistent tabloid room

yacht floats on 80 proof
those breezes
one woman's heaven
is another's vain equestrian confusion
hamper stovepipe love
riding the spelling of the syllable
a word for beautiful
in French masculine
shelter we connipted over rent check
every bristled angel uncorked
bottles of her rage
tipped and poured into white empty face
empty with death
whose plastic surgery refined
an image of perplexity
the fossils very winded
have incorporated planning
into every feeble motion
left within the will
the color *jaune*

hear reasons imperfection
will remain the status quo
a love affair impulsiveness
first branched
toward the desired fraction
of loom thread
twined the other way
tension released
new tension loaded
into half significance
rain the status quo
paunch carburetor
in the truck bum luck
girls very country western
in their way of mentioning mea ever maxima
guilt multi denominational
a grain incapable of quite sustaining
chastened by a permanence
incited by demand
lofty as twin gravity
sensational within a season
opposite

response is very tidy
nod for instance
echo what she's spoken
she has stated helpline
every corporate
oblique wool avenue of change
things back to pretty
if the word once cared
collected tips of iceberg
to be banded into freezer paper
finely tuned electrocution
in someone's image likeness
glandular endorsement
treetops lead to wind
whose core apology tempts freedom
to absolve itself of definition
and suppose to be still
could be likely
several and thoughtful incidents
as private as summer stealth

casual with words
lace picnic
features open curtain
bristled sage pacemaker
alcohol in sufficient quantities
begins to temper love
your family has for you
allotted mainstream bone structure habitat
the normal curve
bathing elaborately night
a fact day lily
stubble ruckus who's the bird
appears to preach headlong white sentences
into a cup
the ownership of instruments
become a sex to call your own
and hound the talk show hosts
with plenty virtue and descriptors
sanctimonious until they fit
complicit strictures

club of trailer park what ifs
lined neatly across verisimilitude
screams of nasturtiums
the body examines
from a scientist position
highlights minutiae
clean up of streets
refusal to be blurred awhile in them
splay further choice cicadas
fracture any clear white
burgeoning of comfort
favor dismal enough rotundas
at the cost of championing nine irons
very neighborly in case of sleep's
logical presence
by the swimming pool
where tension literally cooked
explains a sample of its history
to muscular appearing shadows

shock absorbers don't exist
the body various in places
sense of monotone
though crimson fractions
an oblique surface performance
ecosphere
could brine mandala winehook
harm the loom outrage
she apprehends
skip-stone papyrus mention
in the heroine eclectic duststorm
kipper Heimlich plum
maneuvering the capital
all planned for paisley
spatial as elastic wind
the artificial excess sunrise
peers from dumpling fronds
insinuated lovely
until promenades
become no better than whim
or shame elastic telephone
connective borderline
comforts aimless placement
some way engaged

patio contains
my perfectly relaxed
due chapters
often a composite
silk and wood blend
vulnerable to smudging
of the rafters
inside consequence a fraction
healing anti-symphony
we trespassed on some years
nowhere on record
certitude like that
small town memorabilia
requiring new paint
to be apprenticing
toward fresh lean strokes of gravity
to the power "n"
alias black hole
perfectly concentrated
sleeps with grief until
the grief is rendered powerless
divulged by center light
provided naturally without face
and again enamored

echo chamber fortitude
and expert longing
chivalry collapses
with the flood imperative
brass apple
to hold down the papers
with a life close by
awaiting jigsaw breakage
how many vowel sounds
bicycle their way
to home run particles
when the collective memory
centrifugally ventures
in a tailspin mode
collapsed before
initials reach
the miniature square emblem
dark circles crowded space
beneath the eye
and ink enough to separate
alarm clock from closed blinds
cherished and stick on
like the whittled bloom

logic mostly snatches birds
from every audience
they stipple envy
the pronunciation of tattoo
street clogged with whores
now clean and blank
a has-been office
cylinder appeasement
like the farm
say something
like tape measure
itself
bake white ham
call rabbit carry wish
the foot
and term it luck
buy tickets for the lottery
win mild sachet
to put in nylon drawer
wear proudly even though
the company that sells them insists
on misreading "Dr."
and always
addresses your invoice "Sister"

saint comes co-dependently
to manufacture guilt in me
the out-to-lunch sign
bravely showing in my window
mea culpa be a gentle
ever priest
the coma I am thinking of
arrest record and silence
how the umbilical sum begins
to choke adulthood
without paying attention
health used to be selfish
she cut off body parts to prove
the serious implant of old wounds
fractured
as trombone appears religious
the shorn appearing residue
each volume probable lapdog
genuine pronounceable and free to vary

natural as iambic pent
the family orchestra
for whom composers browbeat staves
or bleed them
to fulfill external urge
to have a purity emerge
sans temperature
beyond predictable enumerated outcomes
offering a reason for umbrellas
or removal of the cotton layers
feigning skin
as every tissue
ultimately descends
to sheer moss
peelable unmissed
finally history
burrow powered in curiosity
ripened by transitive verbs
of calendar that litter pathways
where we legislate
new methods of occurring
in the world
first mentioned randomly

hysterical post-rain mockingbirds
sound lost toward midnight
I sit between silk indoor plant
and an expensive lamp
so warm that I pronounce arthritis dead
the walls contain no spawned art
but what I calibrate on site
from the folding chair to mimic
masters yet unborn
who will dissolve
the canon for a version
plenty sentiment warm carpet
dry moonlight stops being Romantic
Cuba is a song
is to be sprinting over
touched up blacktop dallying
with open air a sought possession

virtually pinned to incapacity
he notices without distraction
guestbed brittle sexuality
gnawing hunger for hard tack
itchy woodsy planetary get lost
where the javelina roam
blind to our fear of them
and lunging circumspectly
because out of balance
see how nourishing
even wind can be
an off night
the cicadas
proving ownership of spaces
to which we apply
the metal tape measure of obligation
sorting what is recommended
from plantation obbligato
twiddling musical enough thumbs
false fronting luminous calamity
alias nature

heal every synonym proceed
with now breathe
do not allow a thing
to clog the passage
present into present
seen always sterling
windshield clarity
inevitable mirror as in any perfect wealth
hands mostly in tune
collect the shards
of what once was
and put them back
into releasetimewholeness
permanent appearing
even blasphemous
enough to replicate some spurious devices
mention snowflake
and I'll pressure you to let go
tease
you seem most comfortable being
is a heady liftoff sans return

accept then weave the center
into body nerves emotional
weave graphic litmus
mention this foremost snapshot
rendered masterpiece
whose pure contralto melts all
sex and urgent armor
dying for significance
whose rope and chime
define the fanfare of a neighborhood
whose swingsets cheapen kinaesthetic jamboree
squeaks liven the yard and sacrifice
of purity as canon echoes
what the elders thought worth saving
in mindrealm charitably rendered
mindloom fastens new craft
to pathways previously unsigned
and kept sequestered
broadjump talent
permanent rehearsal

warzone makes temperate peace
enclosure value foremost
nicotine stained kneecaps
now syllables relax
do pander to the history
of storm awhile
prior to chiseling
new space connective pliancy
the venom capable evaporation
canvas mental mental history
ties your garden apron spoonful
quake once then suppress
the ever laughter glands at ease
the rush now Eden
with a war museum
projected vitriolic headgear
visualize the entropy then further
evolution
grind to a halt no gears
natural sway
a penance
quiet for warlords

about gleams happily from theory
people in swimming invent again a glass
that will accomplish
no release of thirst but will protect
bare vulnerable feet
who bleed
they bleed us lightly
intrigued by sentencing
sequester moon
disturbance shaved around
mayoral battle never interesting
the palace quite infested
with the wrong worms to go fishing
second guess the catch
remark about its presence
in multiplication tables
safety of this house
new rosewood between pen and carpet
plenty solidified to form
new tapestry

sore tributaries rearrange themselves
the mother lode in present tense
how briskly come
the sideboard textures
holy miracle
a spree of evanescent brim ballet
comes the corresponding lime
sequester paperweight
is god the elbow room
is god the baked Alaska
god ice storm near desert
god the inner quiet self distributed
cement unleavened sacrament
rotation
words in themselves possess
sufficient muscle flexibility connects
to rigid motion
as if dance were parody of light
and light stood often still
awaiting dance form

try to build game
into the game
try to function positively
a pass at nudge or cherish
solemn as a block of wood
smile muscles plenty soft relaxed
the television shouts leering obscenities
with blades in them
at empty mouths
seeks identity a cavern
tattled biography
expressive health
burgeons in vitro
the thermostat is low
will rise
swing hammocks
in daisy motion
to the rhythm of red clay
as the sacred can displace a prayer
and hold it gradually
toward center

running water the philosophy
equates to parched land sediment
enclosed particle breathing
for the non-terrestrial worrisome
brand name apocalypse
sufficient ink to persuade others
this is happening
the war on scant resources
motorcycle jacket defining closet
as the fundamental cave
until it echoes expert system
is then ever replicated
in the segregated closets of America
who rule out shawls of nuns
masculine ear muffs
and the pea coat of a trench man
laboring to earn distinction
without capacity to sell it

wake to disrobe night
menace my skin
sufficient thyroid supplement a pleasure
what I think
privately beside you
keeps refusing to accept decoded
version substitute for majesty
abbreviated cross of starlight
with a menagerie
the set jaw grinding
tables of dried ink
until someone massages me awake
I find I battle
the inevitable wordless war
outside of context
if context warranted
consists of an antagonist
and spectators who confuse themselves
with what they watch
and watching start to claim
their due

her rights illuminate
in airline version
lately intoned "eliminate"
50% comprehension of discrimination
between what seem now homonyms
equality the focus
not to be confused with same
she retorts
scourging conceptual dissonance
a multicolored rain
which drop is superior to all others
how to sequester particles of such kin nature
is every pregnancy result of breeding
she asks pointing to stump
infested with insight bearing mushrooms
quoting over the counter axiology
laced with "why is poison
the most trustworthy of elements"

ocean is healthful wine
is healthful music
generally healthful travel
healthful spirituality never in moderation
healthful a commitment to didactic focus
healthful beard an insulation
the protector
a commensurate abundance
come and share with me
my monkcell made for two
is ultimately healthful
prayer is lying still
thought such as the only heart
in two is until separation
stops each making sense
ocean and land are sky and ferment
honesty appreciation sidebar
of the only music is beyond
only the music

ideogram
notes of the scale
coat hanger
do you take this pinesmell
fairly dilapidated trailer
I mean motor home
to be your permanence
this wisp of cell condition
breathing through the nose and mouth
the gateway slow paced
leftist correspondence
course waitlisted
heap of grandeur
lingering design curve
mention handmade woodwind instrument in France
you'll have an argument
concerning reeds and bailing wire
red to contend with
what do you make of
one mascara colored sock
left in the middle street

I sit alone at table
own this afternoon
viable symmetry
free to learn nothing
wheeze exhale
attempt to second guess routine
of nether weeks already threatened
by too slim philosophy
to dare breach the code
avoid a mathematics
veer away from God the subject
chasten physics with simplicity
a change deserves new bulb
only the way this day is kept
will feel surrounded by the urge
to keep it current
by the time it's seen
shows charter gray
as photo album

possible use of energy possible park
a likely upkeep
of less deprecating flowers
than are singed by rigid heat
whose silence finishes the glow
on stem those blossoms
not kin altercation anyway
nor leafy shade
all kinds of parking lot
deplete the story
of personality become milk
pulsed veinward moistened earthtones
a form of bread clock
similarity untoward ephemeral
brand spanking new desk blotter
thirsty as golf green
still shaped skin of simulation
newborn advantage pendularly
draped across
once empty rooms

chance equal chance
centrifugal amenity
new water thinking plunge
suppress
survey Roget's Thesaurus
count them
forty-seven different words for limp
effective tease
you verify my altar
has behind it spirit God
not ancillary whiplash
gathering chilled coin
for maybe days
when weather is a fool
defines itself
too handsome to be functional
and fails
for hobby entertains
wristwatch limits to our growth
who wants anyway excessive evolution
recalls white elephant
pepper enough colored to depress
paprika over chicken
inspiring moderate indulgence

early morning verse
the godlipped heresy
conundrum spoken anxiously
burns headings onto stratosphere
some mothers favor anger
as a way to cleanse
rid greed from every pseudo angel
who would handgrenade unknowingly
then seek forgiveness
be the enemy awhile
heal as the mention of lone grief
perimeter of change
anger is choice
a relic movie brave enough
to be the focus and displacement
to fraternize with guests by our employees
remains strictly forbidden
also consuming
anything within the lounge
then driving

the rate of speed time passage
courage to define philosophy
orbit and genius
science religion hope
the helpless guru chairlift
for the mental physical gone numb
agreement piano tuner
piano mover
pianist in final form
the evolution harmony
played barefoot syndrome
mostly true wallpaper
dramatic chords blueline
spaghetti plants feed therefore hemisphere
a satchel wavers
and slim flag reminisces trees again
the limestone pinched nerve of us
paints open places
veteran blond ancient enough
a product or a permanence
philanthropy assuaged

nouveau instruments
with fiber optics
shift the balance power
when maternal moments happen distantly
transform talk through mistakes
plenty unforeign
hatchet rules and make them
survival in a wooded beauty
here is what the pioneers repeat
of emptiness
it looks the same as full
without some centuries
hors d'oeuvre sized decades
poke a sacred flag in
where it is supposed to mean
thanksgiving suddenly
the natives incessantly putter with tradition
lovingly someone is born to reverence
despair or an unmoved mentality

sends memorandum with the singular
in place of plural
and unreasonable request
I put a bookmark in my flowervase
and go home
the mountain is still shining
island furnishes identity awhile
guitar like a splayed harmony
rich butter cream
folk hit a backwash
latticed garden
quicksand near-term memory
cultural offering
wooden gate prediction
probability exact science
Schenectady my fictive sister
tone poem
grant a four-day hall pass
to the choke chain
to be curdled gold
atop an upright dresser
chastity intact

junk drawer surfaces
after we smudge completely
the new home
sans incident
blessing away war
lukewarm
we heard while mazed
to wall's being
stripped of its function
turned to passageway
curled smoke tonight
led promenade
in the direction of the place
those things uncategorized
will ever lie
matches and smudge
key ashtray
and coin
grocery receipts
mace
glue
barbecue timer
problematically catch vertical drapes
each time they're opened
focus divinely splayed
with smoke the tuning fork
portrayed
in sacred smooth alignment

indebtedness tips guilt
swish nearly to the full abrasive
right face
where sir
I am yes sir
taking your orders sir
all the while aware of grief
the color
grief the touch
and grief the template
sacrosanct enough to breach
a blender salvo
do you take this core apostrophe
to be your signal of intrusion
certain acquiescence
winking tissue farms out aim
and misses crucial lines
that once were segments
then extended their opaque domain
grew clear enough to follow
blended

practice makes the thing
unseen not dead
think for example space in house
to fit the words
as thought
a kind of manifest plum tree
eventful wind when rising
has the radish not so sharply noticed
this is not a hot day
quiet table
this caloric moment life
this faking urgency
to blur obvious pleasure
raison d'etre purity sketched perfectly to scale
repeated toward its disappearance
mimes convey a chortle
simulate motel room emptiness at home
tuned muting party down
impulse

little to point out
to an electron
so an evening off means
distance
from the loved processes
green eyes pasture like
until the insulated enemy
comes forward to receive
unjust dosage of love
to plant the seed
of an unfairly new and improved planet
for his hammock and drug habit
well fed on the miseries
of a big world neighborhood
unspeakably untidy
senseless as guitar stroked
by failed accounting fingers
who unluckily believe
in every proper stroke and stroking
without counts

white walls sift rosary
from digestive system
I have contributed attention span intact
birds of prey are carnival
there's always some excuse
for topers who venerate
their own chapped lips
believe the next binge
will cement into eternity
into repeated drunk prostration
before the statue of saint *carpe diem*
syllables that flow
will fasten to the air
extend to mean
each canon will be left complete
forever
circumference of restitution
will be dumbstruck
no sin exists
full absolution
is a gift

intimate what lasts
the legal definition
rent control inheritance
a license to exist
be entity
a barrier who qualifies
lay down your life
sculpt well thought out alternatives
blood pressure diminishes
with choice
the scars of a romantic charm
sweet knowing bones
this treetop atraditional
warm velvet natural stream
a pulpit crashes to the floor
glued shelving
where a glass of water
and the several leaves
are tucked in preparation
to be scalded
patch of intermediate black hole
entrenched form gravity

bandaid core jalopy
flute a closed hole
engine brim
or treble wanton fist
glorious mystery
aimless this smear of bead
hampering laundry
feel of brimstone
fire
the preacher
ache to breathing
shutters block
the only hope
or curtains elbow out the light
a comfortable posture
gelling as soft glass
rubs against a spectacle
and borne wind learns
calypso who foretells
such clear tones
unless coping demeans itself
to art and craft
at last grows silent
as the stem within snow frictions

trousers and holster with tools
very functional
this home healed
and intimidate
point of unnatural
casting a pot redemption
the elements hardened
to form them into objects
worth possessing
our home
is a crop
and my body
sleeps late here's the movie
I'm living in silence
apology flute speech
coarse animal hair
of the bow on this fiddle
serene as all coupons do flow
so disarmingly
value unburdens itself
of the dailies
and charm redistributes
its potting soil
over scarred surface

bundle of sticks
fumble for matches
history equals primary kindling
chapter verse tea ceremony
why sexism colludes along
the bridge of "in"
secretes endorfins following
brutality
unjust relief I voice
a version protest
thick position paper
very starched looking diploma
sheepskin reveals the fade of shallow wall
adjust intentions
architectural as pomp
the literature of impairment
clarifies
when to have done so little
boosts the stream of memory in wicked key
the strop pituitary vengeance
as in god the omnipresent hormone

inspires regret
the muscle of lead pipe
simultaneously read about a purity
in India namely
bathe the enemy in unconditional love
bowl resonant with light
the color of a chapter
I would treat gestures
uncommonly complex to untangle
warty little hedonist
who shimmied up the corporate greased pole
on someone else's wits
about to fall
teach self no response
the empty swimming pool
a fact of spectacle
the dry dry afternoons without relief
relentless air conditioning
exceeds even
the muscle expectations

digital clockface summons me
on signal "10:05"
childhood address
I may be thinking then
some cure for maternal grief
it comes waving suggestive energy
in my wide open face
consider the masseuse
whose full bruised body
sacraments her craft
as innocence enduring actively this world
athletic fingers
nothing accidental about cold
pressed oil
slathered across
tight muscles of the lower back
that yield tuned answers
to unasked questions this cool canvas
is to be your world
what will you name it

Sheila Murphy's other books include *With House Silence* (Stride Press), *Sad Isn't the Color of Dream* (Stride Press), *Obeli: 21 Contemplations* (Pygmy Forest Press), *Memory Transposed Into the Key of C* (Mochersatz Press), the forthcoming *18/81* (Gesture Press), and a forthcoming book from SUN/gemini Press. In 1990 she participated in the Chax Press Residency program along with Gil Ott, Leslie Scalapino, and Karen Kelley. Some of her recent work has appeared in the magazines *Aerial*, *Avec*, *Big Allis*, *Chelsea*, *Generator*, *Lost and Found Times*, *Paper Air*, *Salt Lick*, and *Tyuonyi*. She lives in Phoenix where she works at the University of Phoenix, plays flute, and co-coordinates the Scottsdale Center for the Arts Poetry Series.